CONVER

CASANOVA

How to Talk to Women, Flirt Like a Pro, and Create Magnetic Attraction

MATTHEW SCHNECK

The information provided herein is stated to be truthful and consistent, in that any liability, in terms of inattention or otherwise, by any usage or abuse of any policies, processes, or directions contained within is the solitary and utter responsibility of the recipient reader. Under no circumstances will any legal responsibility or blame be held against the publisher for any reparation, damages, or monetary loss due to the information herein, either directly or indirectly.

Respective authors own all copyrights not held by the publisher.

The information herein is offered for informational purposes solely, and is universal as so. The presentation of the information is without contract or any type of guarantee assurance.

The trademarks that are used are without any consent, and the publication of the trademark is without permission or backing by the trademark owner. All trademarks and brands within this book are for clarifying purposes only and are owned by the owners themselves, not affiliated with this document.

TABLE OF CONTENTS

CHAPTER 1: BREAKING THE ICE WITH STYLE

Crafting unforgettable opening lines

Kicking off a conversation with impact sets the tone for memorable connections. Your opening line is your chance to grab her attention, spark intrigue, and open the doors to an engaging interaction. Mastering this crucial skill transforms you into a conversational wizard capable of wowing women right from the start.

This chapter reveals the secrets to crafting unforgettable opening lines that get conversations flowing smoothly. You'll discover proven techniques to:

- Catch her interest with creativity and confidence

- Infuse humor and playfulness into your approach

- Make your introductions feel natural, not forced

Rise Above Boring Pleasantries

Let's start by retiring overused openings like "Come here often?" or "What's your name?" While benign, these fail to make a distinctive impression. We can do better. The key is leading with lines that amuse, surprise, or captivate her imagination.

For example, if you spot a woman reading at the park, try opening with, "Let me guess - that book has a plot twist on page 47 that changes everything." This playful prediction grabs attention while inviting her to engage.

Humor also helps you stand out. If you see someone trying samples at the frozen yogurt shop, approach with, "Quick - what topping combinations should I avoid at all costs?" Now you've piqued her curiosity and made her smile.

Crafting Unique Compliment Openers

Heartfelt compliments also make winning conversation ignition. But skip the cliches like, "You have beautiful eyes" - they feel insincere. Instead, pay attention to details others overlook.

Maybe you notice a woman wearing a necklace with an unusual charm. You could start with, "My sister would love that owl necklace - the jewel eyes are so lively and fun." This shows you really saw her personal style.

Essentially, look for openings that feel like they're crafted just for her. This lays the groundwork for an interaction that seems fatefully meant to be.

Channel Your Authentic Self

While gimmicky pickup lines might work on occasion, don't make them your go-to. Leading with sincerity and self-expression breeds better connections.

Tap into your hobbies and interests to fuel engaging openers. For instance, if you're an amateur photographer, you could tell the woman browsing old film cameras, "I can't help but give you photo shoot suggestions - that light over there would highlight your eyes gorgeously."

This tactic leverages your genuine passions while paying a sincere compliment. When you lead with authenticity, conversations flow effortlessly from the first words.

Using situational cues for natural conversation starters

Starting conversations with complete strangers may seem intimidating. But it doesn't have to be with the right techniques. The key is learning to transform your environment into the perfect wingman, priming natural dialogue through situational cues. This chapter unpacks the savvy skills needed to effortlessly craft conversation launch pads from your surroundings.

Scanning for Inspiration

The first step is tuning into your landscape. Scan your scene, noticing standout elements that could act as conversational kindling. Maybe you're at a bustling cafe. Spot someone with a flashy laptop sticker? Bingo

- easy tech chat starter. Catch a glance at an unusual tattoo? Instant inked-skin compliment opener.

Your goal here is gathering quirky environmental details that feel specific to this moment. These become bridge topics to fluidly kickoff chats.

If nothing eye-catching pops out initially, broaden your scope. Eavesdrop on close-by conversations, see what your target and her friends might be discussing. Doing so allows you to organically join an existing dialogue stream.

Crafting Situational Openers

Once you've harvested conversational seeds from your landscape, transform these into personalized openers. This displays social calibration and wit.

For example, maybe you overhear the woman beside you planning a Greek vacation. You could start with, "Greece is on my dream destination list too - any islands you'd say are must visits?"

Or if you notice her dog's leash has your favorite band on it, go with "I have to ask...what's your top song from The Killers?"

Essentially, lead in showing you're tuned into specifics about her. This lays a connection foundation rooted in observational awareness rather than contrived gambits.

Exuding Confident Delivery

Smoothly integrating situational details into openers also requires self-assured delivery. You want to avoid seeming overly excited or eager to force a conversation.

Strike a balance between friendly composure and playful confidence. Smile warmly when approaching but let your body language remain relaxed and open.

Time your opener well too - jump in when there's a lull in her chat so you don't interrupt. Finesse these nuances right and your environmental openers will flow charmingly.

Soon you'll be crafting natural conversation launch pads on the fly anytime, anywhere. Your surroundings will transform into wingmen providing the perfect icebreakers for effortless connections.

Intriguing questions to spark instant rapport

Master conversationalists know the power of intriguing questions for cementing bonds quickly. Strategic inquiry conveys sincere interest while uncovering commonalities to kindle an affinity. This chapter reveals how to craft queries that spark mutual understanding and instant rapport with new acquaintances.

We'll unpack tactics for:

- Asking magnetic questions that pull people in

- Integrating engaging follow-up questions

- Guiding conversations into connectivity

Curiosity Fuels Connections

Cultivating genuine curiosity is key for rapport-building questions. Approach interactions with an explorer's mindset - you're there to discover her landscape of passions, quirks, and perspectives.

Let your curiosity guide query topics too. Maybe something unique on her bag catches your eye. Ask about the cool patch and where she got it. Such interest in her expressions breeds affinity.

Equally valuable are questions revealing worldview overlaps. If you both love hiking, ask about favorite trails or gear must-haves. These queries cement bonds through shared experiences.

The Art of Follow-Up Questions

Skilled conversationalists also flourish by integrating follow-up questions artfully. These display active listening, provoke deeper insights, and further stoke mutually intriguing dialogue.

When she tells you about her recent trip to Nashville for example, don't just reply "Nice." Ask what drew her there, what top highlights she'd recommend, or if the nightlife met expectations.

Such attentive follow-up questions make people feel truly heard. And hearing fosters human connection quickly, even between complete strangers.

Guiding Toward Common Ground

As your rapport-igniting exchanges flow, pivot conversation toward discovering overlapping passions and outlooks. These shared interests act like magnetic attraction forces pulling you closer.

If she's really into obscure indie bands for instance, ask for entertaining music stories. Was she ever in a band herself? Did she road trip hours to a concert? Has she discovered any hole-in-the-wall venues with phenomenal atmosphere?

Soon conversation meanders toward mutual experiences like finding your identity through music and chasing artsy adventures. Bonds solidify rapidly when life outlooks align.

By blending engaged curiosity, thoughtful follow-up, and common ground exploration, your questions become chemistry catalysts. You transform from strangers into kindred spirits crossing paths serendipitously.

CHAPTER 2: BANTER, JOKES, AND PLAYFUL TEASING

Using humor to create emotional connections

Humor builds bonds quickly by catalyzing feel-good chemicals that prime affinity fast. This chapter dives into using playful banter, witty jokes, and charming teases to spark emotional connections through laughter and levity.

We'll explore strategies to:

- Infuse playfulness into initial interactions

- Craft jokes and banter personalized to her

- Tease charmingly without causing offense

Playfulness Opens Doors

Fun is inviting - people gravitate toward experiences that rouse joy and amusement. Harness this principle when initiating conversations by leading playfully.

Maybe you ask a woman waiting in the lengthy coffee shop line to play an imagination game about the baristas' off-duty lives. Or invite someone browsing cereal options to debate the definitive ranking for each box.

Injecting such playfulness into openings signals you'll be an enjoyable companion. Like a mental dance card, her mood meter gets marked with "fun potential" upon meeting you.

Customized Jokes Build Bonds

What really wins hearts is humor tailored specifically to the person you're captivating though. Avoid generic jokes - instead create punchlines pulled from observational details about her.

If she's sporting a t-shirt featuring a whimsical unicorn for example, you could quip about starting a petition against the unfair portrayal of unicorns in mainstream media.

Essentially, flaunt your wit through comments that display how uniquely fascinating you find her. This lays groundwork for an inside joke-rich relationship budding with intimacy.

Charming Teases Done Right

Teasing done well also massively amplifies attraction by blending playfulness with challenge. But ineffective attempts fall flat or offend, so heed this advice.

Keep teases focused on playful assumptions rather than personal criticisms. For example if she orders the triple chocolate lava cake, jokingly warn you now have blackmail material confirming her rebellious side.

Additionally, keep teases light-hearted by smiling warmly and holding relaxed, open body language. This ensures your playful challenges land as flirtation, not attacks. Master both principles and your humor becomes emotional superglue.

Fun teasing tactics to build attraction

Few flirtation methods captivate interest like fun teasing paired with charm and wit. Tactical teases blend playfulness, spontaneity, and harmless mischief - an irresistible allure. This chapter unpacks the art and science behind teasing done endearingly to amplify attraction.

We'll explore strategies for:

- Crafting playful assumptions as fodder for teases

- Infusing teases with charm and positivity

- Balancing sincerity with spirited challenges

The Allure of Playful Assumptions

The key to captivating teases begins with making charming assumptions about her - declarations you playfully pretend are facts. For example, upon meeting a well-dressed woman at the museum, you might tease,

"I know your secret - you're here to steal ideas for your own avant-garde fashion line!"

Teases like this engage imagination and position you as someone attuned to her interests who "gets" her. But assumptions said sincerely without smiles would seem odd. So ensure your body language, tonality, and flair signal harmless fun.

Bouncing Off Reactions

Observe reactions to gauge if your teasings hit the attraction sweet spot. Playfully push back if she refutes your assumptions with banter like "Methinks the lady doth protest too much!" This lively back-and-forth builds bonds quickly through laughter.

But if she seems uncomfortable, soften your tease's impact by pivoting to a thoughtful question or compliment. This realigns your rapport while still retaining playful overtones.

Essentially, let her reactions guide whether to dial teasings up or down accordingly. Soon you'll intuit precisely how much spirited challenging builds attraction best.

Blending Sincerity with Playfulness

Also avoid coming across as trying too hard to impress with your teases. Overly eager efforts feel disingenuous. Instead, infuse teases with authentic appreciation for someone's unique attributes.

For example, if you meet a woman passionately describing her volunteer work overseas, you could tease, "You seem way too adventurous to be happy just working a desk job! I bet you'll be jet-setting on your next global escapade soon." Blending playful assumptions with sincerity hits attraction sweet spots.

Get creative, keep things light-hearted, and ensure she feels respected, not diminished. Do this and your charm-laced teasings will delightfully amplify intrigue and captivation.

CHAPTER 3: STORYTELLING CHARISMA

Painting pictures with descriptive words

Descriptive writing immerses readers deeply inside fictional worlds by painting multi-dimensional scenes overflowing with sensory details. While compact prose has its benefits, vivid passages that stretch moments into technicolor stop motion captivate attention. Like panning a camera slowly across a lush landscape, compelling sensory description offers portals for escape. Master scene-setting through purposeful, poignant word pictures that engage the imagination.

Appealing to the Senses

Rather than merely relaying dry plots, guide readers through experience by depicting environments, characters and objects texturally. Help them feel summer's humid weight, hear concerto crescendos swelling, taste minty moonlight cocktails, sense silk robes cascading over skin. Activate sensations through inventive metaphors and specific imagery that plays minds like cinema screens. Great description generates brain activity lighting up neural pathways. Transport readers sensuously.

Spotlighting Specifics

Once establishing overall mood, zero in on telling details that reveal deeper meaning and themes visually. Maybe a scar traces the main character's hidden vulnerability, peeling gold wallpaper reflects fading fortune, or an unmade bed symbolizes relationships deteriorating behind closed doors. Unique elements lend poignancy; eschew cliches. Sprinkle these throughout to sustain intrigue rather than cramming at the chapter's start. Spread crumbs tantalizing readers to actualize your fictional place fully.

Structuring Spatial Dynamics

Orient readers within settings through accurate spatial awareness choreography, noting characters' positions, scene geography and transitions across locations. Establish cardinal directions to prevent disorientation during motion. Utilize blocking to heighten suspense and power dynamics by leveraging proximity and positioning. Does the argument intensify with adversaries squaring off toe-to-toe? Positioning molds engagement.

Inviting Investment Through Immersion

By crafting scenes specifically textured for readership demographics, emotional investment deepens through relevance. Know intrinsic motivations driving fans to this genre then incorporate visceral details and symbolic elements amplifying associated wishes, fears or aspirations. Does suspense hinge on urgent justice so foreground earthy weapons? Romance on reclaiming feminine power through lavish gardens? Heightening signature desires forges bonds between worlds.

Vivid writing grants eyes that not only envision words but taste, touch and enter your world through sensory portal. Will you build doorways inviting the intoxicated immersion reading offers? Mind the gap between paragraphs to welcome wanderers inside.

Shaping compelling narratives

Narrative remains one of humanity's most primal technologies for making meaning of life's chaos. Even in modern times, the irresistible pull of story continues enthralling hearts and minds. By learning what makes tales truly compelling across genres and formats, we better spark that ancient alchemy between words and souls that transforms readers forever through wonder and cathartic wisdom.

Defining Clear Story Architecture

Just as sturdy houses require engineering support beams, impactful stories need structured framing to elevate content. Outline crisp logline summarizing the plot, protagonist, obstacles and outcomes in 1-2 sentences. Establish themes woven throughout each narrative element underscoring core messages. Sketch timeline milestones of inciting incidents escalating into climactic showdowns then falling action resolving central conflict. Visible architecture gives creative freedom.

Developing Dimensional Characters

Even the most meticulously plotted stories fall flat with superficial characters. Ensure protagonists and antagonists possess clear motivations, distinct voices and developmental arcs revealing transformations over time. Explore backstories shaping worldviews through traumatic formative events and resulting wounds carried into their quests. Vulnerability humanizes. Craft supporting characters highlighting alternate angles on your themes to create compelling discourse.

Seeding Mystery and Suspense

Layer in intriguing unknowns across exposition, inciting incidents and progressive complications to pique reader curiosity hungry for answers. Foreshadow subtly through symbolic imagery and prophetic dialogue emphasizing not knowing destinies ahead. Build cliffhangers making outcomes uncertain when chapters close or seasons finale. Suspense emerges from the gaps between what is seen and unseen. Leave breathing room for imagination between narrative strokes.

Elevating Stakes and Tension

Raise continuity risks making threats feel more imminent, failures more devastating in their consequences. Shorten timelines forcing hurried decisions by those ill-prepared. Remove safety nets like income, community or health creating perceived checkmate scenarios. Push characters outside comfort zones through power reversals. The higher the climb, the harder heroes crash or triumphantly overcome.

Make it personal through relationships, dignity and growth on the line.

Great stories reveal both human and divine—mirroring life's essential questions through plots reflecting who we are, why we suffer and how we might walk with hope. Will you tell truth unflinchingly? The world awaits tales only your heart knows.

Making ordinary stories extraordinary

Injecting Wonder into the Mundane

Life teems with overlooked stories. Peer closer at apparent ordinary days and micro-dramas ripe for spotlighting. Even routine harbors hidden currents of comedy, intrigue and beauty when viewed aslant. By magnifying facets of common experiences often dismissed as unremarkable, skillful storytelling transforms the banal into extraordinary for readership hungry to encounter the strange vitality imbuing all things.

Noticing Backdrop Wonder

Train observational skills on frequently ignored urban and natural environments surrounding characters, showcasing eccentric details easy to miss when only focused on plot unfolding in the foreground. Catalog telling specifics like "stray cats gathered by trashcans like patchwork quilt squares" or "rainbow smeared sky behind the bank's gothic silhouette." Creative nonfiction especially thrives on elevating unnoticed beauty now symbolically reframing story meaning.

Cherishing Character Nuances

Illuminate quirks organically revealing dimensions beyond initial stereotypes. Maybe the brash athlete privately volunteers at animal shelters. The mousy librarian once dreamed of Broadway. The graceful dancer battles chronic injuries. Write against type by spotlighting secret passions, unlikely backstories and subtle complexities demonstrating all souls' remarkable depth once you honor hidden facets. Everyone carries wonders unseen.

Finding Whimsy in the Workaday

Even repetitive jobs and institutional environments seethe with peculiarity and humor for those keen-eyed enough. Send observant protagonists on adventures interacting with eclectic coworkers or navigating bureaucratic escapades ripe for satire. Catalog lingo, customs and colorful company hierarchies. Exaggerate limiting rules and dysfunction toward fantastical ends. The conjured magic of Dilbert or The Office lives on.

Grounding Fantasy in Emotional Truth

While heightening reality toward strange horizons, ensure exaggerated elements nonetheless tap into universally felt hopes, fears and meaning so readers relate intimately. Does the zombie apocalypse represent anxiety about mortality? Aliens symbolize desires to belong? Vampire immortality a wish to conquer time and loss? Successful fantasy elevates, not eliminates, poignant humanity. Even surrealism reveals our deepest truths.

Great alchemy emerges from transmuting the ordinary into extraordinary through loving attention — reminding jaded eyes trained only to expect life's mundane dusty greys just how shockingly beautiful and miraculous this world bursts when illuminated aslant with radiant intention. Will you reveal the shy glory hiding in all things?

CHAPTER 4: EMOTIONAL INTELLIGENCE IN ACTION

Reading body language cues

Decoding Nonverbal Communication

Beneath spoken words often lies a hidden language transmitted through fleeting facial expressions, gestures, posture, proxemics and tone. By tuning into these nonverbal signals, we bypass social masks to intuit true emotional states and interpersonal dynamics at play. Learn body language fundamentals to sharpen social awareness and better navigate relationships.

Understanding Common Cues

Catalog frequently observed mannerisms and micro-expressions correlated with specific moods to accurately assess behavioral implications. For example, sustained eye contact, smiling and open limbed gestures signal receptiveness while crossed arms or leaning away conveys distance. Recognize that multiple simultaneous cues provide more context than any single isolated sign. Consider combinations holistically before reaching conclusions.

Reading Beyond First Impressions

Look beyond initial reads, remaining cognizant of cultural and personality variation in displaying emotions comfortably. Some demonstrate freely while others disguise feelings. Consider context too when interpreting intent - stressors impacting behavior or baseline temperament masking objective state. Withhold quick character judgments as first perceptions may falsely cast innocent styles as suspicious simply because they contradict social norms or our own projection.

Noticing Incongruent Messaging

When verbal language clashes dramatically with body language, focus primarily on physical leakage rather than honed speech easily manipulated for masking authentic state. Fidgeting motions, repetitive grooming gestures and posture shifts often betray discomfort levels despite cheerful façades. However, understand that inconsistent messaging may also indicate internal conflict rather than deception. Explore sensitively rather than accuse.

Considering Motivations

Before assigning assumed positive or negative intent behind another's behavior, hypothesize possible root motivations compassionately. Does the coworker avoiding eye contact struggle with anxiety rather than disengagement? Is their curt tone unintentionally mismatched to context rather than anger? Might crossed arms signal insecurity not defiance? Generously interpreting reasons behind actions prevents reactive contempt prior to investigating thoughtfully first.

Tuning Into The Eyes

As windows into emotional and mental experience, eyes offer direct pathways into the soul if we dare gaze at them directly. Notice eye movement patterns - whether steady or fluctuating during conversation. Simultaneously, observe pupil dilation as it reveals interest and receptivity levels. Gaze patterns communicate volumes. Locked eyes mutually exchange vulnerability when met heart-on-heart.

By balancing nonverbal observation with graciousness for multiple interpretations, we forge bonds through dissolving divisive barriers. May a spirit of deep listening guide all explorations toward unity.

Tuning into her feelings

Despite social conditioning urging masculine restraint, learning to attune sensitively to women's rich inner lives fosters mutually fulfilling relationships. Gaze beyond surface moods into subtler emotional landscapes many dismissal as mere melodrama. Approach feelings as portals for deep listening rather than problems to rapidly fix. By forging an empathetic connection around her experiences, you strengthen trust in the sanctuary all souls crave.

Recognizing Emotional Complexity

Avoid belittling intensities by appreciating feminine emotions as multilayered messages received more acutely due to biological and cultural factors. Consider monthly hormonal fluctuations or exhaustion from constantly vigilant threat scanning taught since girlhood. Understanding contexts explains reactions; ask how she feels and why with sincere curiosity to know her world.

Reading Signs of Overwhelm

Notice early nonverbal cues suggesting emotions approach overwhelming capacity, from clenched jaws to wringing hands. Even slight irritation in those habitually gentle may indicate inner turmoil. Calibrate your own response to match rising intensity levels through compassionate silence rather than criticism. Reflect her sentiments back genuinely before inquiring what she requires next in that moment - advice, distraction or hug.

Exploring Meanings and Stories

When she shares vulnerably, recognize tears or anger rarely reflect surface provocations alone but rather accumulate from unresolved pain collecting over weeks, months or a lifetime tilting her axis askew. Avoid diminishing significance by instead asking what old wounds current situations agitate. Trace connections through each memory, heartbreak and lesson learned. Emotions gain sense once threaded to origin stories.

Holding Space Without Fixing Allow expansive expression without rushed analysis. Witness and validate before questioning "why" endlessly or strategizing solutions. Reflect what you heard in her own words. Ask what she needs, resisting the urge to prematurely soothe, downplay or redirect from messy pain in discomfort. Tolerating intensity passes this too;

strong hearts grow stronger still through loving presence not erasure of their truth.

By honoring the intricate terrain of women's emotional worlds, men transcend conditioning that judges feeling to embrace sacred wholeness waiting below surface tension. In selfless listening blooms the door to oneness.

Displaying empathy and understanding

In divisive eras, choosing basic human kindness emerges as radical defiance against indifference. Yet empathy lives innately inside all our hearts, awaiting activation through moral courage. By relearning skills strengthening compassion's muscle too often left to atrophy, we rediscover sacred bonds linking lives beneath surface divisions. Shared suffering calls us home into the solace of mutual understanding all souls intrinsically seek.

Humbling Personal Perspective

Catch yourself projecting stories onto strangers rather than knowing truth. Notice when interpreting their behaviors, beliefs or cultures through a lens fogged by personal assumptions about acceptable conduct. Consciously acknowledge the limits of partial views shaped by upbringing. Make space for realities outside your own without judgement. Curiosity invites truth; arrogance breeds illusion.

Suspending Snap Reaction

Train patience for knee-jerk responses like criticism, disgust or contempt when encountering alternate worldviews - especially related to oppression or privilege blind spots. Pause internal monologues long enough to ask clarifying questions with sincerity, not accusation. Seek first to understand rather than demonize, playing devil's advocate toward nonjudgmental middle ground. Breathe before reacting.

Finding Common Ground

Once hearing someone's experience, highlight shared sentiments you recognize in own life to build bridges from. "I also know the feeling of..." or "Your story reminds me of..." opens doors. We all experience anger, heartbreak, alienation, vulnerability and hopes for belonging. Name those universal threads that tether our humanity despite surface variation in circumstance. We stand on common ground.

Speaking Experiential Truth

Verify intellectual knowledge through lived experience - the courageous choice to immerse in actual scenarios evoking empathy. Volunteer serving marginalized communities, read diverse authors' stories told raw from the trenches, take the homeless person out to lunch. When hearts stay open to strangers' and loved ones' very real suffering up close, denial about injustice withers through humanizing those labeled "other."

Before judging righteousness, first pull the log from your eyes to clear vision clouded by ignorance. Befriend truth through humble seeking. In compassion breathes divine reunion with all living beings across perceived divides. Therein unfolds heaven on Earth.

Chapter 5: Compliments and Observations

Sincere praise and appreciation

Division threatens human bonds in eras where technology connects yet isolates. Stubbornly believing you alone grasp truth while others wander in ignorance breeds hatred. Yet when we open hearts to diverse perspectives, common ground emerges. The courageous choice of compassion builds bridges across apparent divides to rediscover shared hopes and struggles defining our inextricable humanity.

Cultivating Curiosity Over Contempt

Train yourself to approach alternate worldviews with sincere curiosity rather than knee-jerk contempt when encountering opposing ideologies or unfamiliar cultures. Notice how personal assumptions fog clear assessment, acknowledging inherent limits in grasping nuanced experiences outside your own. Ask honest questions free of implied superiority to understand different vantage points before judging righteousness. Therein wisdom dawns.

Walking Empathetic Miles

Intellectual knowledge lacks impact without investing tangible effort experiencing scenarios evoking compassion. Choose to read marginalized authors' stories from the trenches, volunteer aiding underserved communities, befriend a homeless neighbor. When privileged insulation cracks through humanizing society's invisibles as equals, denial about injustice withers. Hearts remaining open to strangers' suffering hold hope for paradigm evolution.

Finding Common Ground

Despite surface variations in identity or beliefs that trigger defensive reactions when egos feel threatened, search deeper for painful universal experiences all share—love, grief, anger, isolation, loss. Catalog voiced sentiments you recognize from your own seasons of hardship. "I too know how vulnerability/rejection/uncertainty feels..." builds bonds. What we suffer reveals inextricable threads of humanity binding us.

Pausing Before Demonizing

When encountering worldviews drastically diverging from your lens on ethics or oppression, resist the magnetic pull toward hatred as cross-cultural misunderstanding often unintentionally breeds harm. Suspend condemnation long enough to ask clarifying questions with sincerity, not accusation. Play impartial advocate gently illuminating blind spots. Where possible, highlight shared values underpinning polarized stances. Therein connection waits.

May we ever lift the torch of compassion to see beyond walls that divide us into the light of sacred unity awaiting when souls truly see each other. There unfolds heaven on Earth.

Noticing details others miss

The wonder of ordinary life unveils fully when we study environments and interactions with an explorer's mindfulness releasing preconceived blindness. By cultivating intense presence without distraction, eccentric particulars overlooked by casual glances astonish eyes and hearts awakened to beauty's subtle details glinting all around. Sharpen perception to uncover hidden miracles within the mundane.

Scanning Scenes Slowly

Commit to truly seeing spaces through sweeping eyes across entire visual fields rather than jumping quickly to focal points like faces or reading material. Let atmospheres imprint fully before assessing experience. Wander landscapes inside houses and city streets alike noting small delights easy to rush past like sunbeams aslant on chair cushions or intricate architectural embellishments overhead. Pause often to soak in details.

Deepening Sensory Awareness

Listen and feel environments as well as gaze at them. Tune into background sounds - rustling leaves, footsteps echoing from around corners, the electric hum of appliances. Distinguish scents riding breezes through open windows - rain, pine trees, grill smoke. Tracing stimuli through multiple senses amplifies immersion in present moments where secrets hide.

Appreciating Quirks and Whimsy

Observe fellow humans with the same open wonder that delights in nature's oddities. Catalog people's charming idiosyncrasies - music teachers conducting phantom orchestras, children inventing sidewalk games, elderly couples bickering then tenderly kissing. Allow your heart to swell with affection for all these wondrous beings bumbling through existence together on this spinning globe. Find the endearing in all souls.

Uncovering Hidden Symbolism

Study environments, conversations and behaviors for deeper meaning cloaked subtly in metaphor. Does the violent thunderstorm mirror explosive tensions building elsewhere? Do two neighbors' remarks about fences hint at secret rivalry? Flags at half mast foreboding tragedy on the horizon? Like reading poetic literature between bald lines, contextual clues reveal intriguing backstories once you adopt a spirit of playful interpretation.

Great secrets hide in plain sight for those committed to rediscovery's joy. May you resurrect childlike astonishment that unfailingly drinks in beauty otherwise eclipsed by assumption and routine. Our world unveils wonder and magic ceaselessly for awakened eyes.

Uplifting comments done skillfully

Here are some tips for offering uplifting comments skillfully:

- Be sincere. Don't offer fake praise or say things you don't genuinely mean. Make sure your intentions are truly to lift others up.

- Be specific. Rather than a generic "good job," name details that resonated positively with you. This shows you really noticed and underscores why you appreciate their efforts.

- Focus on strengths. Avoid backhanded compliments about weaknesses. Keep the spotlight on celebrating positive qualities you admire.

- Consider timing. Make sure your comments are sensitive to the situation and won't seem tone-deaf. Reassuring someone they did their best after a tough loss requires more care than after an easy win.

- Use uplifting language. Say things like "I appreciate how dedicated you are," "You handled that situation beautifully," "Your calm leadership carried us through." Communicate warmth through word choice.

- Check assumptions. Don't project desired traits onto people that don't resonate with their truth. Comments like "you're so unfazed by anything" may cause dissonance for those privately struggling.

- Inspire growth. Note small improvements over time. "I've witnessed how much more patience you've cultivated this year." Progress, however subtle, fuels self-efficacy.

The key is ensuring your positivity comes across as authentic encouragement rather than empty flattery. Skillful support nourishes others' spirits.

CHAPTER 6: FLIRTING MASTERY

Playful touches and smiles

Flirting involves more than just talking - using appropriate body language and physical touches can take your flirting skills to the next level. Subtle, playful touches and smiles are powerful ways to create a flirtatious connection and build attraction.

Light, fleeting touches are an excellent flirting technique when used appropriately. A gentle touch on her arm when you're emphasizing a point or laughing at something she said shows your interest. Or, if you've been chatting for a while, a light touch on her shoulder or back as you guide her to the bar or dance floor helps make flirting more physical. Even just briefly touching her hand or fingers when you hand her a drink helps create sparks of attraction. The key is to start slow with brief, innocent touches and gauge her reaction - if she seems comfortable, you can gradually increase the duration and intimacy of the touches. But avoid touching her too early before rapport is built or touching areas that might make her uncomfortable. Keep it friendly and fun.

Playful touches like gentle pokes, nudges, and pats on the arm or back are also great for flirty teasing. For example, if she playfully teases you, respond with a poke on the arm and a witty comeback while holding eye contact and smiling. This shows you can take a joke and keeps the playful vibe going. You can also try gentle tickling or squeezing her hand when you're laughing together. Just take care not to overdo it - you want to flirt, not annoy. Keep it light and read her signals.

Smiling and eye contact work hand-in-hand with touch to boost flirtatious attraction. Warm, genuine smiles show you're comfortable, having fun, and interested. Smile when you first catch her eye from across the room - a confident, low-key smile is inviting without being creepy. Hold her gaze for a couple seconds before looking away and starting an approach. Smile again when you introduce yourself and make a witty comment to get things started. Don't forget to keep smiling periodically throughout your conversation to maintain an upbeat, fun vibe. Laughing together is also a great way to get closer. And when you're both laughing, that's a great time for playful touches like a nudge or squeeze on her arm.

Coy, flirty smiles are also effective when combined with a look-away. For example, smile directly at her as you're talking, hold her gaze for a few seconds, then look down shyly and smile before glancing back up. This creates a "secret smile" vibe that subtly signals your interest without being too overt. Similarly, you can try the cute crooked smile - smile at her as you look down and away, showing just a hint of that crooked smile. Time it just right when she says or does something cute - this shows you're both amused by and attracted to her.

It's important to smile naturally rather than just grinning constantly like a creepy clown. Relax your face and smile subtly at opportune moments when you feel genuinely amused, happy, or interested. Don't force it - think of fun or flirty thoughts and allow your natural smile to emerge. If you feel nervous or self-conscious your smile will look awkward. Mentally focus outward on HER, not inward on yourself. Making HER happy and smiling is what will make your smile look its best.

Mastering playful touches and smiles takes flirting finesse. But when done right, combining gentle physical contact with warm, genuine smiles sends a clear signal that you find her attractive and enjoy being close. Just remember to read her signals, start slow, and don't overdo it - you want her smiling back, not calling security. With practice you'll be creating sparks and connection in no time.

Captivating eye contact techniques

Making strong eye contact is one of the most powerful ways to connect with someone and show confidence.

When done right, your eyes can communicate interest, attraction, authority, and more. Master these captivating eye contact techniques to mesmerize and allure.

Lock Eyes Across the Room

Want to get someone's attention from afar? Use the lock and release technique. First, lock eyes with your target from across the room. Hold the gaze for 3 to 5 seconds, giving a slight smile if it feels natural. Resist the urge to immediately look away. After a few seconds, slowly release the eye contact and casually look around the room. Then repeat by locking eyes again. This builds anticipation and shows you're interested but not desperate.

The Triangle Technique

When talking one-on-one, create a triangular gaze pattern between their eyes and mouth. Make eye contact for a few seconds, briefly glance down at their mouth, then return to their eyes. This subtle triangle creates a tantalizing flow of eye contact that won't feel intimidating. Avoid staring at their mouth too long - just quick little glances to keep things spicy.

Linger Longer on Laughs

Want to show you enjoy their company? Linger your gaze a bit longer when they laugh or smile. Don't just glance away immediately - really soak in their smile and laugh along with your eyes. This communicates warmth and appreciation for seeing them happy. Just don't overdo it or you'll seem entranced. Three seconds of extra eye contact on laughs is perfect.

Gaze, Look Away, Gaze

Here's a move that builds anticipation. While chatting, hold eye contact, pause briefly, then look away toward their mouth or elsewhere on their face. Hold for a few seconds, then reconnect your gaze. The brief break will intensify the eye contact when you lock eyes again. Do this a few times, mixing up the duration of the breaks.

The Sideways Glance

Next time you're nearby one another, like sitting at a bar, try the sideways glance. Casually turn your body slightly away while turning your head to make eye contact. Hold for a second, then slowly turn your head back. This subtle head turn catches their attention and sparks curiosity. Feel free to add a slight enigmatic smile as you turn back around.

Eye Contact While Speaking

When talking, balance eye contact with looking away. Maintain eye contact while making your main points, but break contact when providing context or lighter info. This draws focus to what you want emphasized. Don't just stare non-stop - that's creepy. Regular eye breaks keep things comfortable.

Responsive Eye Contact

Eye contact isn't just about technique - it's also about responsiveness. Observe their eyes and body language for engagement signals. If they maintain eye contact, they're likely interested. If they seem distracted, break contact to relieve pressure. Reflect their interest level - don't force it if they're disengaged.

Slow It Down

A common mistake is rushing eye contact. Don't just rapidly glance at their eyes sporadically. Make slow, purposeful eye contact. Take a full second or two to really focus in on their eyes, smile, then slowly release. Quick glances feel nervous - linger longer to mesmerize.

Practice, Practice, Practice!

Like any skill, captivating eye contact requires practice. Try these techniques the next time you're chatting with someone you want to impress. Challenge yourself to maintain strong eye contact despite feeling shy. Over time, holding eye contact will start to feel natural, comfortable, and even exciting! Just remember, focus on connecting, not dominating. Your eyes should be engaging, not overbearing. With a spirit of friendly confidence, you'll master the magnetic power of eye contact in no time!

Charming body language and gestures

Your body language reveals more about you than you realize. Mastering charming, magnetic gestures and movement is essential for making great first impressions and sparking attraction. Follow these tips to ensure your body language amplifies your charisma.

Stand Tall, Chest Out

Confident posture is foundational for charming body language. Avoid slouching or crossing your arms, which conveys closed-off discomfort. Instead stand tall with your chest slightly out, shoulders back, and arms relaxed at your sides. This projects an approachable yet authoritative energy. Aim for upright but not overly stiff.

Lean In Slightly

Leaning your upper body slightly toward someone signals engagement and interest. But beware of leaning too far and invading personal space. Start with just a subtle lean of a few inches when conversing, pivoting your torso rather than whole body. Read their body language - if they reciprocate leaning in, you can accentuate it more. If not, avoid aggressive leaning.

Tilt Your Head

A slight head tilt to the side comes across as warm and thoughtful, like you're truly listening and interested in what the other person is saying. Keep your chin level - don't tilt up or down. And use the tilt sparingly for emphasis rather than keeping your head permanently cocked.

Smile With Your Eyes

Charm isn't just about your mouth - it's the whole face. When smiling or laughing, let it reach your eyes. Crinkle your eyes sincerely, lifting your cheeks. Eye smiles communicate joy and enthusiasm. Practice smiling in the mirror so it looks and feels natural.

Open Gestures

Keep your hands open and visible, not hidden or clenched. Have palms face up or outwards rather than down. Unbutton coats and roll up sleeves to avoid looking rigid. When gesturing, use open palms rather than pointed fingers which feels aggressive. Open hands are a sign you have nothing to hide.

Occasional Touch

Subtle yet thoughtful body contact builds connection. Examples include a light touch on the arm when making a point or gently guiding them through a crowd. Focus on brief touches of the forearm, upper back, or shoulder. Ask first if touching their lower back so you don't invade their space.

Mirror Their Movements

Syncing your body language helps put others at ease while building mutual rapport. For example, if they lean in, reciprocate by leaning in closer yourself. Or if they gesture frequently, loosely mirror their rate of gesturing. Avoid mimicking them move for move like a creepy impersonator. Just reflect the same energy.

Confident Gestures

Convey confidence through expansive gestures. When talking, avoid fidgeting. Instead, hold your hands in front of you with palms up. For emphasis, try open palm-up gestures. Point your finger upward when making a good point. Wide, sweeping gestures also captivate attention.

Take Up Space

Rather than collapsing inward on yourself when standing, occupy your entitled space. Adopt wide stances rather than keeping your feet together and arms crammed at your sides. Uncross your legs when seated.

Claiming your personal space displays dominance and confidence.

Relaxed Movements

Avoid looking rigid and anxious. Maintain composure with smooth, fluid motions. Nod your head naturally as others speak. Keep your torso loose and gesticulate smoothly rather than jerky motions. Take up space when stationary but move with elegance and control.

With these tips, you can fine-tune your body language to naturally attract and influence others. But remember, charm stems from genuineness. Don't force gestures or expressions. Focus on openness, confidence, and interest in those around you. With practice, charming body language will become second nature.

CHAPTER 7: VERBAL SEDUCTION TACTICS

Insinuation and innuendos done artfully

Mastering the art of insinuation allows you to subtly communicate sexual interest and build tantalizing romantic tension. Dropped at the right moments, innuendos and insinuations grab attention, excite imagination, and amplify attraction without being crass. Learn how to artfully craft alluring verbal foreplay.

The Indirect Approach

Good seduction follows an indirect, subtle path. Blunt statements about what you want to do come across as creepy and aggressive. Instead, make layered remarks open to interpretation. For example, respond to a woman's playful teasing by saying "Ooh, feisty, I like it" with a wry smile. This hints at your interest without overtly stating it.

Ask Thought-Provoking Questions

Questions that get imaginations stirring are perfect for insinuation. If you sense chemistry, lean in close and ask "Have you been bad or good lately?" in a low playful voice. Let her mind wander interpreting your intent. Or if you're discussing weekend plans, ask "What's the craziest thing you've ever done on vacation?" Her answers give insight while building sexual tension.

Use Ambiguous Adjectives

Descriptive words like "hot," "steamy," "racy," and "adventurous" are ideal innuendos. If she mentions a fun trip, respond "Ooh, sounds stimulating" with a suggestive eyebrow raise. Or describe an attractive woman as "spicy" or "vivacious." By inserting sexual undertones into benign conversations, you stoke curiosity about your true desires.

Flirt With Your Voice

It's not just what you say but how you say it. Lower your vocal pitch slightly and speak slower and softer to make benign phrases seem intimate. Add breathy pauses. Say her name in a drawn out, sultry way when greeting her. Compliment her hair by first smelling it and going "Mmmm" for a sensory insinuation.

Use Playful irony

Irony allows you to say things indirectly while hinting at more. If a woman is getting handsy, take her hands gently and say "Now now, behave yourself young lady." This playfully implies you don't really want her to behave. Or if she suggests hiking, respond "Just hiking? That sounds boring" to spark exciting hypotheticals.

Have fun layering innuendos and insinuations into conversations to build thrilling tension. Be subtle - you want to stoke their imagination, not shock them. The art is in how much is left unsaid.

Alluring language patterns

Language can entrance and excite when selected carefully. By incorporating alluring speech patterns into everyday conversation, you can mesmerize women without seeming overly seducing. Subtle sexuality in communication kindles imagination and deepens connections.

Vocal Volume Variation

Monotone voices bore. Instead, vary your vocal volume to create an almost musical dynamic. Lower your volume gradually when sharing something confidential, drawing her in. Increase volume during humorous stories, amplifying the humor. Soft and loud vocal tones add texture.

Thoughtful Pauses

Well-timed pauses build suspense between statements, forcing her to anticipate your next words. After saying something mildly provocative, pause briefly before continuing. This imbues your words with promise and importance. Don't overdo it - one or two second pauses are enough.

Open-Ended Questions

Asking open-ended questions encourages detailed, revealing responses. Simple yes/no questions halt conversation momentum. Instead spark discussion with questions like "What's your most treasured childhood memory?" This provides insight into her values and personality.

Compliment Unique Traits

Anyone can generically praise beauty. But highlighting unique traits and quirks communicates you notice nuances about her. Compliment a distinctive laugh, funky style choice, or quick wit. Specificity shows genuine appreciation rather than empty flattery.

Make Statements, Not Questions

Confidently making thoughtful statements signals assertiveness and conviction. Too many questions can seem wishy-washy and insecure. Provide opinions, share observations, and make declarative statements rather than constantly saying, "Don't you think?"

Sensory Descriptions

Engage the senses with details and descriptions. Discuss music in terms of rhythms, scents as sweet or musky, cocktails as smokey and peaty. Loaded language excites imagination. Just keep it classy - no gross graphic descriptions.

Revealing Desires

Sharing desires and daydreams feels intimate and bonding. Say things like "I've always wanted to go to Thailand and dive off coastal caves" or "My dream is to publish a great American novel one day." Avoid trite cliches - make it meaningfully personal.

With attentiveness and practice, you can develop alluring communication habits. Just take care that your allurement elevates conversation rather than dominates it. Speak to spark imagination, not solely stimulate.

Intriguing vocal techniques

Your voice and vocal delivery carry enormous influence. Beyond your word choice, the quality and modulation of your voice can mesmerize and deeply connect with listeners when honed. Practice these intriguing vocal techniques to add compelling dimension to your everyday speech.

Vary Tone and Pitch

Monotone voices tend to bore and drone. For lively interaction, consciously vary your tone, pitch and inflection. Lower your vocal pitch when sharing something confidential or serious. Raise it to elevate excitement in happy stories. Inflect upwards at the end of sentences to encourage response.

Thoughtful Pausing

Well-placed pauses add suspense and emphasis to your words. After making a meaningful statement, pause for 2-3 seconds before continuing to allow the meaning to sink in. Resist nervous babbling - embrace thoughtful silence. Pausing before responding to a question also makes you seem considerate rather than hasty.

Enunciate Clearly

Mumbling and muttering under your breath conveys anxiety and lack of confidence. Instead, speak clearly and articulate every word, paying attention to tricky sounds. Enunciate endings like "ing" rather than trailing off. Crisp, clear enunciation makes you sound thoughtful and self-assured.

Lower Your Volume

When you want to intensify intimacy in conversation, lower your vocal volume gradually. This draws her focus in and makes her lean closer to hear. Just don't get so quiet she can't hear you at all! Find the sweet spot where she must intently listen while you maintain vocal presence.

Infuse Playfulness

Don't forget to have fun with your voice! Warm, playful vocal tones are utterly captivating. Smile as you speak to naturally liven your voice. Allow your excitement or laughter to fill your voice when appropriate. Sounding happy and upbeat keeps conversations light and engaging.

Embrace Silence

Some of the most intriguing voices know when not to speak. Allow pauses in conversation while maintaining eye contact and facial expressiveness. You don't always have to rush to fill dead air. Silence gives your voice more impact when you do use it meaningfully.

Record and Review

Many people dislike the sound of their voice until they grow accustomed to it. Record yourself and replay to gain awareness of vocal habits. Identify areas needing improvement. Track your progress getting comfortable with your unique vocal qualities.

With presence and practice, you can mesmerize others through your voice. Remember, compelling speech flows from inner confidence and genuine connection. Master these techniques, but focus on authenticity rather than just allure. Your distinctive voice already has immense beauty and influence when used with purpose.

CHAPTER 8: DEEP RAPPORT AND CONNECTING

Stimulating her mind

Great seduction transcends the physical to truly stimulate the mind. Avoid superficial small talk and generic compliments. Instead intrigue and connect on a mental level through creativity, imagination, and sharing philosophies. A woman craves a man who can both challenge her mind and understand her at the deepest levels.

Share Passions and Hobbies

Don't just stick to resume talk. Dive into discussing activities that energize and fascinate you. If you love vintage jazz, explain what moves you emotionally about those smoky saxophones. Let your enthusiasm for photography or surfing reveal your zeal for life. Ask follow up questions to engage her passions too.

Debate Playfully

Playful banter and debate build rapport fast. If she professes a questionable opinion, challenge her with a witty counterpoint. But keep it fun and smile, don't attack harshly. Say she claims pineapple doesn't belong on pizza - gasp in mock offense and argue your contrasting view. Just don't let it escalate into real conflict.

Discuss Meaningful Topics

Transcend superficial topics by broaching meaningful issues. Share your dreams and worldviews. Ask about her life philosophy and values. Have you both always felt like outsiders? That builds an intellectual bond. Just avoid getting too heavy too fast. Keep it thoughtful but with levity.

Compliment Her Smarts

Attractive women get plenty of looks-based compliments. Stand out by praising her brains and resourcefulness. For example, compliment her savvy business strategy or ability to think on her feet. This shows you admire her mind. But focus on skills, not just generic intelligence.

Exchange Reading Suggestions

Asking for and sharing book, article, and video recommendations reveals intellectual tastes. If she's into philosophy, introduce her to Schopenhauer. Ask her to recommend a novel that moved her deeply. Follow up later by discussing your reactions. This intellectual exchange stimulates attraction.

Learn Her Love Languages

How someone desires to give and receive love differs according to their "love language." Some crave physical touch, others quality time. Learn whether she connects through words, gifts, acts of service, or other expressions. Then tailor your rapport strategies accordingly.

The mind is the most neglected erogenous zone. But stimulating conversation builds intimacy unmatched by the purely physical. Challenge, understand, and connect with her mind first - her body will soon follow.

Thought-provoking dialogue

Mastering the art of deep, thought-provoking dialogue communicates your emotional intelligence and ability to connect beyond surface-level chatter. When a conversation turns existential, philosophical, or poetic, rapport intensifies rapidly.

Share Personal Growth Stories

Revealing stories about overcoming challenges shows depth and self-awareness. For example, tell her how you coped when unexpectedly fired and found new meaning by starting a nonprofit. Or discuss moving past previous dating hang-ups to embrace vulnerability again. Keep it real – no exaggerations.

Ask Unexpected Questions

Jolt a conversation out of mundane patterns by asking delightfully unusual questions. For instance: "What would your 80 year old self advise you to do more of right now?" Or, "Which of your personality traits still surprises you?" The unpredictability gets minds whirring in new directions.

Discuss Her Dreams

People open up when you show interest in their aspirations. Ask thoughtful questions about her deepest dreams in life, from traveling the world to starting a family or artistic endeavor. Then share your own hopes and connect over common visions.

Reveal Your Fears

Carefully exposing insecurities forges an empathetic bond. If she shares her fears, reciprocate by admitting one of yours, like failing professionally or never finding lasting love. But avoid being overly gloomy – keep it manageable.

Compliment Her Mind

Praising physical beauty feels shallow. Instead, compliment her vivid imagination, sharp intuition, excellent memory or intelligence. This shows you recognize and appreciate her interior gifts.

Remember, thought-provoking connection should uplift, not devastate. Keep exchanges hopeful and solution-focused. With emotional intelligence and discretion, you'll form bonds astounding in their resiliency and depth.

Discovering mutual interests

Finding common interests builds an instant sense of rapport and familiarity. Rather than sticking to small talk, explore shared passions, hobbies, values and experiences. These overlapping interests reveal compatibility and provide exciting avenues for further connection.

Ask Open-Ended Questions

Avoid questions with simple one-word answers. Instead ask open-ended questions that provide insight into her interests. For example, "What's your absolute favorite travel destination so far and why?" Her expanded answer may reveal common ground.

Name Your Interests and Passions

Volunteer information about your interests and passions to prime conversation. Say, "I'm really into live music - especially jazz and funk bands. I try to catch local shows when I can." This gives her openings to connect if music moves her too.

Do Your Research Beforehand

If possible, do some light research about her beforehand, like checking her Facebook likes and online profiles. This equips you with conversation topics tied to her interests. Just don't be creepy by knowing too much!

Listen for Subtle Cues

Pay close attention even to passing comments that reveal her hobbies and values. If she says, "I'd love to visit New Zealand someday," ask what draws her to that destination. That tiny cue may unveil common wanderlust.

Find Shared Nostalgia

Shared cultural nostalgia bonds generations. Ask, "What 90s songs were your teenage anthems?" or "Who was your first celebrity crush growing up?" Comparing childhood pop culture touchstones stimulates enjoyable reminiscing.

Mutual interests generate natural momentum that carries conversations deeper. Adapt a curious, creative mindset when seeking commonalities. With insight and attentiveness, fascinating overlaps will emerge organically.

CHAPTER 9: DATE INVITATIONS WITH CONFIDENCE

Reading signals of attraction

Before taking the leap of asking someone on a date, it's crucial to read their signals of attraction. Making a move too soon can damage a budding connection. Watch for these subtle signs she's interested and receptive before extending a date invitation.

Enthusiastic Engagement

Does she seem fully engaged in conversations with you, maintaining eye contact and asking you questions? Or does she scan the room or check her phone constantly? Mutual enthusiasm indicates she's attracted and wants more one-on-one time.

Physical Cues

Attention to physical cues like smiling, blushing and mirroring your body language conveys mutual intrigue. Does she stand closer to you than others? Become more animated in gesture and expression? Getting physically attuned shows she "feels the vibe."

Compliments and Teasing

Playful compliments on your appearance, personality or accomplishments hint she's sizing you up romantically. Similarly, light teasing and sarcastic banter are often attempts at flirtation. How do you respond? Reciprocate to keep building rapport.

Lingering Goodbyes

Does she seem in no rush to end conversations with you, lingering longer than necessary upon exiting? This reluctance demonstrates she enjoys the chemistry.

Lowered Inhibitions

As attraction builds, people naturally loosen up and drop some social inhibitions. Notice if she opens up about more personal topics, talks with her hands more, or giggles more frequently in your interactions.

Trust your instincts over formulas. If you genuinely sense strands of attraction interweaving, the time may be ripe. Just ensure signals are consistently mutual before formally asking for a date, rather than acting on a few subtle clues that may merely be politeness. Patience pays off.

Extending exciting invitations

Once you're reasonably convinced of mutual attraction, it's time to extend a memorable date invitation expressing your unique personality. Avoid clichés and be thoughtfully creative, piquing her curiosity and excitement about spending more one-on-one time with you.

Highlight Common Interests

Incorporate shared interests, passions or desired experiences into your date plan based on prior conversations. For example: "I'd love to take you out to this new French bistro I discovered - I remember you saying French culture fascinates you."

Have an Activity in Mind

Skip nondescript invitations like "Want to hang out soon?" Have a specific activity in mind, like checking out a fun new bar with live bands or an outdoor sculpture garden. She'll appreciate you put thought into planning a fun, solid first date.

Offer Flexible Details

While proposing a concrete activity, keep other details open-ended. For example: "I'd love to take you hiking this weekend if you're free. I know a few great trails nearby – let me know if Saturday or Sunday works better for you." Flexibility shows consideration.

Limit First Date Investment

Lavish dates create unrealistic expectations. Keep it casual and low-investment, like meeting for coffee or a drink. Say: "Could I interest you in happy hour cocktails at The Spot this Friday?" Dinner and a movie can come later.

Frame It as an Adventure

Rather than a routine "let's meet up," frame the date as embarking on an adventure together: "Want to join me on an adventure to the new axe-throwing range this Wednesday?" This romanticizes the outing and sets an exciting tone.

With thoughtfulness and a spirit of fun, date invitations become opportunities to begin revealing your personality. Stay flexible while showcasing your interests and creativity. Most importantly, highlight the joy of exploring connections, not just activities.

Planning memorable outings

A thoughtful, unique date plan makes a phenomenal first impression. Avoid boring dinner-and-a-movie cliches and spark her curiosity with these tips for crafting memorable outings that facilitate bonding.

Highlight Common Interests

Show you've been listening by incorporating shared interests into your date. If you both love jazz, invite her to a cool lounge's live show. This demonstrates your attentiveness and gives built-in conversation fuel.

Do Daytime Activities

Save the intimate dinner dates for later. Opt for a daytime museum visit, hike, craft fair or other activity date to foster communication without pressure. Bonus: you get to see her natural daylight beauty.

Plan For Dialogue

Choose activities conducive to talking, like a quirky walking tour, painting date or browsing a bookstore. This provides ongoing prompts to learn about her while sharing yourself. Avoid lengthy movies.

Add Excitement

Incorporate a sense of adventure like kayaking, hiking to a scenic overlook or playing a sport like mini golf.

This energy and playfulness sparks bonding chemistry. Just ensure you both actually enjoy the activity.

Have a Backup Option

Especially for outdoor dates, have a backup activity in mind in case of inclement weather, like catching a local band's concert if the picnic gets rained out. Advanced planning prevents ruined outings.

Getting creative with first dates builds eager anticipation and sets an unforgettable tone. But remember, an elaborate outing can't replace authentic connection. Focus less on "impressing" her and more on facilitating real conversations to nurture intimacy. That's the foundation for lasting relationships.

CHAPTER 10: MAINTAINING HER INTEREST

Fun communication between dates

In those anxious days between first and second dates, many people struggle to keep attraction simmering through communication. Avoid interview-style small talk. Instead, continue cultivating chemistry with playful banter and mental stimulation.

Continue Inside Jokes

If any private jokes or silly references emerged during your first date, revisit them in messages to keep laughter flowing. For example: "How's your pineapple pizza withdrawal going? ;) Need me to smuggle you some?"

Send Thought-Provoking Articles

Don't just stick to "hey how's your day?" mundanity. Share interesting articles related to topics she's passionate about. For example, send a New Yorker piece on Mediterranean travel if she loves Greece. Include a message tying it to your conversations.

Play "Would You Rather"

Keep things fun by posing playful questions like "Would you rather only be able to whisper or only be able to shout for the rest of your life?" Getting a peek into her whimsical side builds bonds.

Discuss Favorite Moments

Fondly reference favorite moments from your date that revealed her magnetism: "I can't stop thinking about how adorably excited you got telling me about your volunteer work - your passion is contagious!" This compliments while making callback connections.

Tease Judiciously

Once you know each other better, gentle teasing can be playfully alluring between dates. For example, jokingly call her out for a questionable movie taste she confessed on the date. Just ensure teasing stems from affection, not criticism.

Your communication style between dates should mirror the real-life chemistry you hope to continue building. Show you're thinking of her, but also keep things lighthearted and intellectually engaging. Maintain thatmomentum until your next rendezvous!

Showing your charming personality

It's easy to seem generically pleasant during initial meetups. But to spark ongoing intimacy, you must reveal unique dimensions of your charming personality through communication between dates. Showcase what makes you special beyond superficial charm.

Share Amusing Anecdotes

Weave funny, relatable stories from your day into messages rather than just trading logistics and small talk. For example, describe an awkward moment chatting with an overly stoic barista or theUpdate typos and improve flow.

Send Handwritten Notes

Stand out by sending a cute handwritten thank-you card after the date mentioning how much you enjoy her company. Your unique penmanship and wording feels more personal than a generic text. Just keep it concise.

Discuss Childhood Memories

Open up by sharing vividly depicted memories from your childhood, like adventures on your family farm or embarrassing middle school moments. Transport her into your world and past.

Text Song Lyrics That Remind You of Her

If you hear a song with romantic or fanciful lyrics fitting of her, text a verse while you're apart: "Listening to Jack Johnson and this verse made me think of your sense of adventure." Swoon!

Compliment Her Quirks

We often minimize quirks on dates, like playful giggles or the way she scrunches her nose. But highlighting unique traits and mannerisms now shows you find them endearing.

The beginnings of relationships thrive on continuously discovering each other's complexities and contradictions. Drop the Mr. Cool persona. Show offbeat aspects of your personality to deepen intimacy during the delicate interim between dates.

Avoiding conversation pitfalls

The communication between first and second dates balances on a knife's edge. While you want to be playful and provocative, many common conversation pitfalls ruin budding relationships at this fragile stage. Sidestep these hazards.

Don't Brag

Avoid long arrogant monologues bragging about your impressive achievements or possessions. A little humility and self-deprecating humor is much more charming. You want a conversational partner, not a swooning fan.

Don't Get Too Vulnerable

Similarly, oversharing your deepest fears, insecurities or emotional baggage is premature. Light disclosure about hobbies, dreams and personality is fine. But hold off on heavy vulnerability or it will overwhelm things.

Avoid Negativity

Conversation downers like complaining about your job, exes, the state of the world or your achy knee ruin romantic momentum fast. Stay upbeat and positive when chatting between dates to nurture the spark.

Don't Overmessage

Bombarding someone with constant texts and memes screams over-eagerness. Mix longer check-ins with some stretches of radio silence to stay mysterious. And don't double text without a reply.

Stay Present

Don't bring up other dates you're going on. Making her feel like just another option rather than special kills chemistry. Give her your full attention when conversing.

Watch the Alcohol

Happy hour banter can breed undesirable over-familiarity. Plus, you want your wits when messaging. Save the drinks for date two.

Conversation is much like flirting itself—it's best when you alternately advance and retreat. Push things forward, then pull back occasionally. Find that balance, and you'll build excitement for the next encounter.

www.ingramcontent.com/pod-product-compliance
Ingram Content Group UK Ltd.
Pitfield, Milton Keynes, MK11 3LW, UK
UKHW030635170225
4624UKWH00035B/389